W9-ARJ-448

A NEW YORK SHA...   ...PRODUCTION

in association with ....ons

Joseph Papp
Presents

A CHORUS LINE

Conceived, Choreographed and Directed by
Michael Bennett

Book by	*Music by*	*Lyrics by*
James Kirkwood &	**Marvin Hamlisch**	**Edward Kleban**
Nicholas Dante		

Co-choreographer
Bob Avian

Setting by	*Costumes by*	*Lighting by*	*Sound by*
Robin Wagner	**Theoni V. Aldredge**	**Tharon Musser**	**Abe Jacob**

Orchestrations by	*Music Coordinator*
Bill Byers, Hershey Kay &	**Robert Thomas**
Jonathan Tunick	

Music Direction and Vocal Arrangements by
Don Pippin

Associate Producer
Bernard Gersten

1. Musical revues, comedies,
etc. — scores
I. Title
II. Kleban, Edward
III. Bennett, Michael

Piano Reduction by Robert H. Noeltner

ISBN 0-88188-011-6

(previously ISBN: 0 8494 0086 4)

A publication of
EDWIN H. MORRIS & COMPANY
A Division of MPL Communications, Inc.

FIRST PERFORMANCE AT THE PUBLIC THEATRE, NEW YORK
April 16, 1975

CAST OF CHARACTERS
(in alphabetical order)

ROY .... Scott Allen

KRISTINE .... Renee Baughman

SHEILA .... Carole Bishop

VAL .... Pamel Blair

MIKE .... Wayne Cilento

BUTCH .... Chuck Cissel

LARRY .... Clive Clerk

MAGGIE .... Kay Cole

RICHIE .... Ronald Dennis

TRICIA .... Donna Drake

TOM .... Brandt Edwards

JUDY .... Patricia Garland

LOIS .... Carolyn Kirsch

DON .... Ron Kuhlman

BEBE .... Nancy Lane

CONNIE .... Baayork Lee

DIANA .... Priscilla Lopez

ZACH .... Robert LuPone

MARK .... Cameron Mason

CASSIE .... Donna McKechnie

AL .... Don Percassi

FRANK .... Michael Serrecchia

GREG .... Michel Stuart

BOBBY .... Thomas J. Walsh

PAUL .... Sammy Williams

VICKI .... Crissy Wilzak

SCENE

An Audition

Time: Now.   Place: Here.

The characters portrayed in "A Chorus Line" are, for the most part, based upon the lives and experiences of Broadway dancers. This show is dedicated to anyone who has ever danced in a chorus or marched in step . . . anywhere.

A CHORUS LINE IS PERFORMED WITHOUT AN INTERMISSION

ORCHESTRA

REEDS:

I. Alto Sax, Flute, Piccolo, Clarinet, Alto Flute

II. Alto Sax, Clarinet, Bass Clarinet, E Flat Clarinet, Flute

III. Tenor Sax, Oboe, English Horn, Clarinet, Flute

IV. Bari. Sax, Bassoon, E Flat Contra-Bass Clarinet, Flute, Clarinet

TRUMPETS I, II, III (All Double Flugelhorn)

TROMBONES I, II, TROMBONE III (Bass Trombone)

PERCUSSION: Timpani, Xylophone, Vibes, Grande Casa, Bell Plate, Bell Tree, Bells, Drums, Harp, Bass (Doubles Fender Bass), Guitar/Banjo

KEYBOARD I: Piano, Electric Fender Rhodes Piano, Celeste

***KEYBOARD II: Yamaha Y-30 Organ + Leslie Speaker
Baldwin Harpsichord (Electric)**

*Keyboard II is played by the conductor.

MUSICAL NUMBERS

A CHORUS LINE

Lyrics by EDWARD KLEBAN

Music by MARVIN HAMLISCH

No. 1

OPENING

Moderato (not too fast)

Cue: From Stage Manager 5 1/2 SETTING ON FENDER; Organ: Preset #1 Plus Pec.

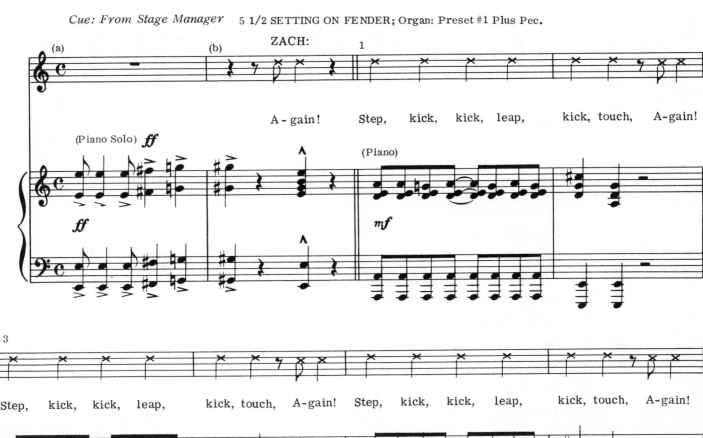

A-gain! Step, kick, kick, leap, kick, touch, A-gain!

Step, kick, kick, leap, kick, touch, A-gain! Step, kick, kick, leap, kick, touch, A-gain!

Step, kick, kick, leap, kick, touch. Right! That con-nects with turn, turn, out, in, touch, step,

6

Turn, turn, touch, down, back, step, piv-ot, step, walk, walk, walk. Right! Let's do

the whole combination facing away from the mirror. From the top, 5 - 6 - 7 - 8 -

New Tempo - Bright in 1

[Vamp]

O. K., let's do the ballet
combination one more time.

Boys and girls   together.
Don't   kill yourselves. MARK!

1 - 2 - 3 -
4 - 5 - 6 -

Ballet Waltz

are second, down,   fourth. I wanna see it.   Again: "1 - 2 - 3 -
4 - 5 - 6 - "

Tempo I

ALL:
Yelled, not sung.

God, I real-ly blew it!

(boys on top)

I real-ly blew it.

ALL:

How could I do a thing like

18

ZACH: Sheila, do you know the combination?
SHEILA: I knew it when I was in front. ZACH: Okay, boys. 5 - 6 - 7 - 8 -

22

. . . 149, 152, 179 - - - Cassie. Other girls, thank you very much for coming. I'm sorry.

(Piano Solo) *f*

rall.

(+Bass)

Slow 2

CUE: ZACH: Boys, - Number 5.....

(Tpts.)

pp

(Piano tacet)

(Sxs. Trbs.)

(Bass) (+Cymbal Roll)

Cut off on Cue

ZACH:

81 and 84. The other boys, thank you.

Tempo I

ZACH: Larry...

(Piano) (+ Organ)

f

dim.

(+Bass, Gtr.)

(Offstage voices continue to sing)

GROUP:

God, I think I've got it.   I think I've got it.

(Almost whispered)

p

That is a pic-ture of a per-son I don't know.

What does he want from me? What should I try to be?

So man-y fac-es all a-round, and here we go. I

need this job. Oh God, I need this show.

"MORALES" - UNDERSCORE

AFTER "THE OPENING"

(The Line)

No. 4

Intro - I CAN DO THAT

I CAN DO THAT

I stuff her shoes____ with ex-tra socks,____ run sev-en blocks.

(Clar. Ten.)

____ in noth-in' flat.____ Hell, I can do that.__

(Cl. Ten.)

(vibes) 8va.

Cm7 Eb6 E7 F7

(Br./Ten./Bar.)

f

(+Gtr.) Bb9 G7

R. H.

L. H. fz

f

____ I can do that!____

(Cl.)

C7 F9 (Cow Bell) (Tpts.) (+Tbns.) Tbn. 1

f

Dance ____

(Cl. Tpt.)

(Ten.)

("RED HOT")

I got to class ____ and had it made ____ and so I stayed ____ the rest ___ of my life. All thanks to Sis ____ (now mar-ried and fat), ____ I can do this. ____

No. 6

INTRODUCTION "...AND..."

40

No. 6a

"...AND..."

44

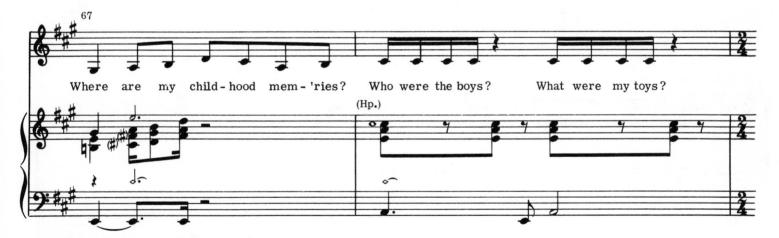

Alternate lyrics for JUDY (measures 64 – 72)

✱ If the actress playing JUDY is not especially tall, but instead is extremely thin:

God, I'm a wreck.
God, I'm a wreck.
I don't know where to start.
I'm gonna fall apart.
Where are my childhood mem'ries?

Who were the boys?
What were my toys?
How will I begin?
And why am I so thin?!!!

✱ If the actress playing JUDY is neither especially tall nor especially thin:

Try to be calm.
Try to be calm.
You're getting overwrought.
Follow a train of thought.
That way you won't be nervous.

Try to relax.
Try to relax.
Only lasts a while.
I'll close my eyes and smile. (Does so)

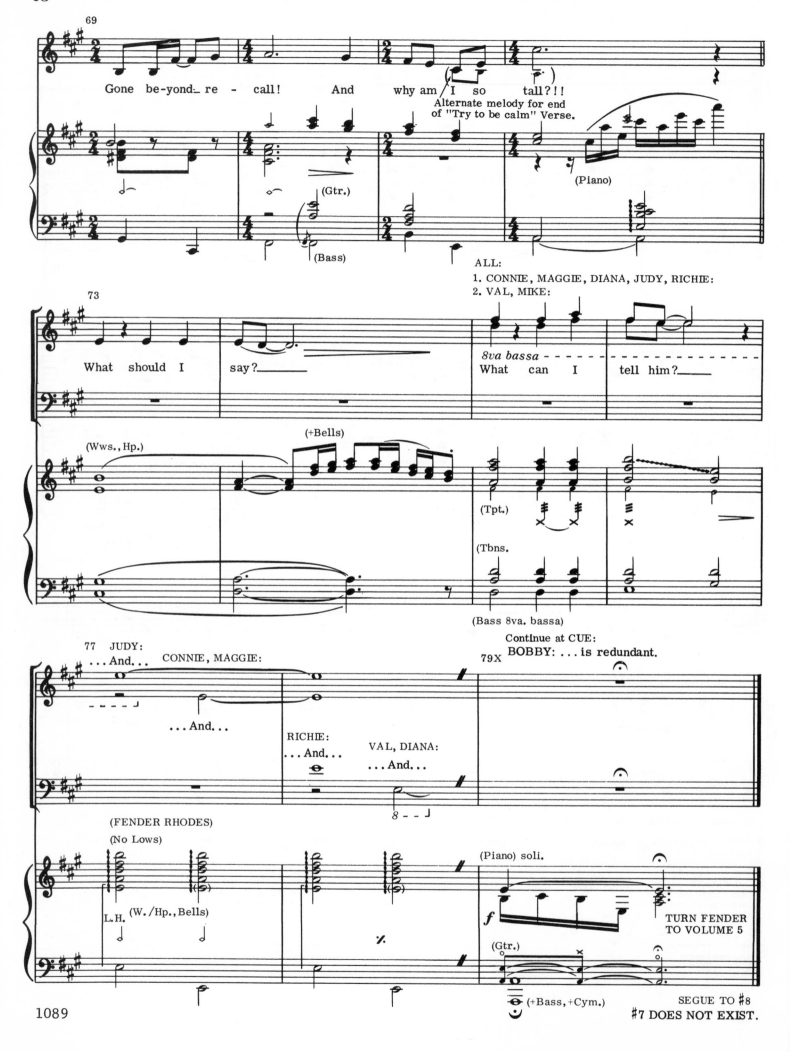

No. 8

INTRODUCTION-AT THE BALLET

No. 9

AT THE BALLET

CUE: ZACH: Sure, you're strong enough. (Begin Vamp)
SHEILA:"Well let's face it. My family scene was not good.

No. 10

INTRODUCTION-SING

CUE: AL: **Tell him how you started.**

AL: "Ed Sullivan"

KRISTINE: It was... oh-right.
Slowly in 2

(Fl., Bsn. -expressivo)

(Vibes, Gtr., Hp.)

(Bass)

(Celesta in octaves)

(Wws.)

On downbeat (KRISTINE: Doris Day.)
During ⌢ "Except I had this little..."
AL: Problem.

KRISTINE: See, I real-ly could-n't

(Fl., Bsn.)

(Vibes, Hp., Gtr.)

(Cl)

(Bass)

SEGUE as one to "Sing"
(Bar 12)

SING !

68

It is so dis-cour-ag... Dar-ling, please stop an-swer...

...-ting. ...-ging. ...-ring!

(Hp., Cl., Bsn., Tbns.)

See, I real-ly could-n't ... I could nev-er real-ly ... What I could-n't do was ...

...sing. ...sing.

(+Ww., Hp., Celesta, Bells)

Più mosso

GIRLS:

GIRLS: KRISTINE:
(off-key)

Do re mi fa sol la ti do. Do ti la sol fa mi re do. La, La,

BOYS:

Do re mi fa sol la ti do. La

(Ob., Cl.)

(Tutti)

(Cl.)

(Tbn. 1)

(Piano, Bs., Bsn.)

(Trb.)

(Drs.)

(+Timp.)

No. 12

MONTAGE - Part 1

("Hello Twelve", Mark, Connie)

Hel-lo Thir - teen, Hel-lo Love.

Next day I went to our doc - tor down ___ the block. Sure e - nough... a -

cute ap-pen-di-ci-tis! ___ They rushed me right to the hos - pi - tal.

Well, I fig-ured this book would cov - er ev - 'ry-thing

drink the wa - ter and I drank like twen-ty glass - es a day.

For three weeks .... I almost drowned ... Finally I went to confession ...

and I told the priest that I had gonorrhea! ... He was in shock, too. "Who have you been with, my

In 1 (Slowly)

son?"("Nobody, Nobody!")"Then how can you have gon-or - rhe - a?"

84

Quickly

(Dialogue)

Picc. solo

(Flg., Hn.)   (Tbn.)

(Pno. tacet)

(Picc.)

(Tpt.)   (Bs.)   (Tpt.)   (Picc.)   (Tpt.)

ZACH: RICHIE: CONNIE:
Ah-hah, the year of the Chicken, ... thirty-two? Puck-puck-puck-puck girl!   So I got   caught! But I don't
Alternate lines for non-Oriental CONNIE.
ZACH:... Thirty-two? I thought you said you were born in 1955. (RICHIE line omitted)

(Cls.)

(Piano)
(Tbns., Bsn.)

(CONNIE:) last time

look it, and I shouldn't knock it,   'cause I've always been able to work.   From   the

SEGUE as one to Part-2

No. 13

MONTAGE - PART 2

("NOTHING")

and it's snowing out. And it's cold . . .

O. K., go!

(Piano) (Sleigh Bells)

Tbns.

(Hp. /Dr s. /Tri. /Tamb.)

Ev- 'ry day   for a   week we would try   to   feel   the   mo - tion,

(Ww., Tpt 1)

(Bs.)   (+Gtr.)

feel the mo - tion down the hill.

Ev-'ry day for a week we would try to hear the wind rush,

hear the wind rush, feel the chill. And I

dug right down to the bot-tom of my soul to see what I had in - side. Yes, I

Sec- ond week, more ad - vanced and we had to be a ta - ble,

be a sports car... ice cream cone.

Mis- ter Karp, he would say, "Ver- y good, ex - cept Mor-a - les.—

Try, Mor-a - les,— all a lone." So I

lowed it, which real - ly makes me burn. They were so

help - ful. They called me hope - less.

Un - til I real - ly did - n't know where else to

(Spoken)
turn! And Karp kept saying: "Morales, I think you should transfer to girls' high. You'll never be an

noth-ing!_____ This course is noth-ing!_____ If you want

some-thing, go find a bet-ter class. And when you

find one, you'll be an act-ress." And I as-

sure you that's what fin-'lly came to pass.

Six months lat - er I heard that Karp had died. _____ And I

dug right down to the bot-tom of my soul .... and

cried, _____ 'cause I felt . . . . .

noth-ing. _____

SEGUE Part 3

No. 14

MONTAGE - PART 3

(Don, Judy, "Mother")

one club for a-bout eight weeks straight and I real-ly be-came friend-ly with this

(Piano +Cls.)

strip-per._____ (Talk) Her name was
Lola Latores
and her dynamic twin forty fours.

(no Cls.)

(Tpt. 1)
Tbns.

(growl)

p

Well, she really took to me. I mean, we did share the only dressing room and

(Cls.)

(no Cls.)

(Br.)

An - y - way, she used to come and pick___ me up and drive me to work nights.

(+Br.)

(no Br.)

(Cls.)

100

SEGUE as one to Montage—Part 4

MONTAGE - PART 4

(Judy (cont.), Greg, Richie)

114

118

No. 16

DANCE: TEN; LOOKS: THREE

... Radio City and the Rockettes,

DICTATED:
I'm gonna dance on ... in the alley with all the ... For dance: Ten.
BROADWAY etc. ... other REJECTS etc. ... For LOOKS: Three. Well,

Tempo: Bright 2

Dance: ____ ten;

(+Sxs.,Tbns.,Rhy.)

(Sxs.)

(Gtr.)

mf

fp   fp   fp

looks: three. ____ And I'm still on un-em-ploy-ment, danc-ing for my

(Gtr., cont.)

(+Bar., +B. Tbn.)   (+Bar.,+B. Tbn.)

own en-joy-ment. That ain't it, ____ kid. That ain't it, ____ kid. "Dance: ____ ten;

(+Xylo.)   (+Sxs.)

(+Bar., B. Tbn.)

VAL: You're all looking at my tits now, aren't you?... *(Dialogue continues)*

SHORT "PAUL" SCENE

Almost SEGUE #18

No. 18

THE MUSIC AND THE MIRROR

CASSIE: a SO-SO FILM ... part ended up getting cut ... etc.

Got to SQUEEZE A ROLL...

I was a dancing Band-aid ... etc.

We had an Earthquake ... etc.

VAMP TILL READY

CUE to continue; CASSIE: I need a job.

...what I should be doing myself.

God, I'm a danc-er, a danc-er danc-es!

Give me some-bod-y to dance with. Give me a place to fit in.

Help me re-turn to the world of the liv-ing by show-ing me how to be - gin.

Play me the mu-sic. Give me the chance to come

146

through.   All I ev - er need - ed   was the mu -

- sic,   and the mir - ror,   and the chance____

to   dance...____

AFTER MUSIC AND MIRROR

No. 20

END OF PAUL'S SCENE

CUE: PAUL: Take care of my son. ... That was the first time he ever called me that.
Starts another line ... breaks down.

No. 21

ONE

CUE: ZACH: "Alright, bring 'em in."

to none,   son.   Oooh!   Sigh!

Give her your at-ten-tion.   Do   I   real-ly have to men-tion   she's

the   one?

(+Wws.)   (To Celesta)

ZACH: (Last time)

5 - 6 - 7 - 8 -
VAMP-if needed

* If played by only one pianist, play indicated Chord Symbols. Play them eerily and dreamily.

197

For the girl is sec-ond ___ best ___ to none,

200

son. Oooh! Sigh! Give her your at-ten-tion. ___

203

Do I real-ly have to men-tion she's

R.H.

206

the one?

178

You know you'll nev-er be lone — ly with you know who.

One mo-ment in her pres-ence and you can for-get the rest._____

For the girl is se-cond best_____ to none, son.

Oooh! Sigh! Give her your at-ten-tion._____ Do I real-ly have to men-tion

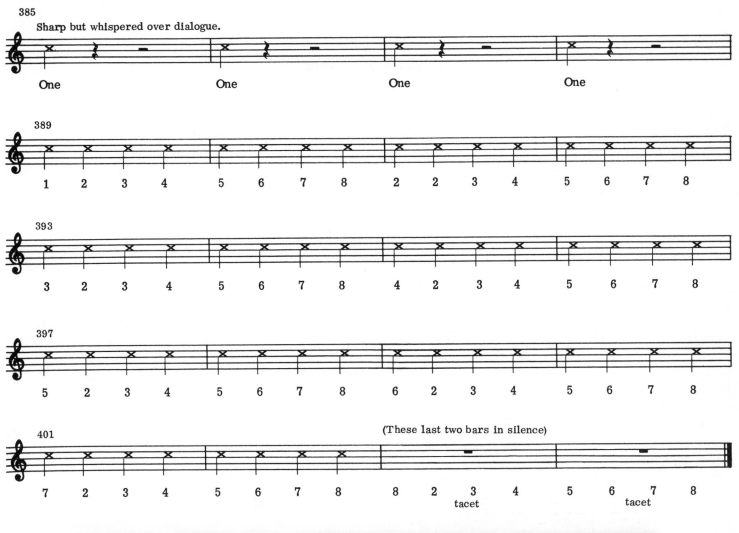

TAP DANCE

190

If George Ham-il-ton can be a mov - ie star, then

I could be a mov-ie star.

What am I do-ing in show busi-ness?

No. 22a

ALTERNATIVES

No. 23

NEW - WHAT I DID FOR LOVE - 1977
(Version "Ab")

No. 24

AFTER–WHAT I DID FOR LOVE

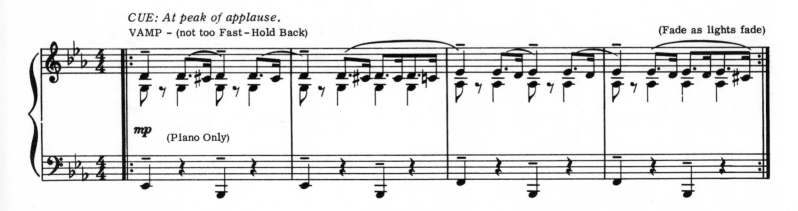

No. 25

BOWS

com-mon-ly rare, ver-y u-nique, per-i-pa-tet-ic, po-et-ic and chic. She walks in___ to a room___

___ and you know from her mad-den-ing poise, ef-fort-less whirl, she's the spec-ial girl.

Stroll - ing, can't help all of her qual-i-ties ex -

tol - ling. Load-ed with cha-ris-ma is ma

76

she is one___ of a kind.

(Brass)

accel.

(Bells)

3   3

New Brighter Tempo

79 BOYS:

One

sin - gu - lar sen - sa - tion   ev 'ry lit - tle step   she takes.

GIRLS:

3   3

She walks in - to a room ___ and you know___ she's un - com - mon - ly rare, ver - y u - nique,

(Cls., Bell Tree)

f (Brass)

82

One

thrill - ing com - bi - na - tion

3   3   3

per - i - pa - tet - ic, po - et - ic and chic.   She walks in - to a room ___ and you know___ from her

(Cls., Bell Tree)

(Brass)

220